Contents

Which cat?

Cats come in all shapes and sizes and some need more looking after than others. Whatever type of cat you get, remember that cats are not toys and should always be treated with respect.

Mongrel kittens born in the same litter might all be different colours. Mongrel cats are often called moggies.

Is a cat for me?

To find out if a cat is the right pet for you, here are some questions to ask:

🐾 Will I feed my cat every day and clean out its food bowl and litter tray?

🐾 Will I take my cat to the vet regularly for its annual injections and check-ups?

🐾 What will I do with my cat when I go on holiday? (Cats cannot be left alone to look after themselves while you're away.)

🐾 Will I train my pet properly and not lose my temper and shout at it?

🐾 Will my younger brothers or sisters treat my pet properly as well?

🐾 A cat can live for about 15 years or more. Will I make sure it is looked after for the whole of its life?

If you answer 'yes' to all of these questions, then a cat could be the pet for you!

Different features

There are many **breeds** of cats and some have distinctive features. For example, Manx cats have a short, stubby tail – or no tail at all. The Scottish Fold cat has ears that fold flat. Longhaired cats such as Maine Coons and Persians have long, fine fur and bushy, fluffy tails. You need to **groom** these cats every day or their fur will get tangled and matted. Shorthaired cats are much easier to look after and don't need to be groomed every day.

Of all cats, the Cornish Rex has the shortest fur. The fur is wavy, and the cat also has short, curly whiskers and large ears.

Know your Pet

CATS and Kittens

Honor Head

QED Publishing

Copyright © QED Publishing 2006

First published in the UK in 2006 by
QED Publishing
A Quarto Group company
226 City Road
London EC1V 2TT
www.qed-publishing.co.uk

A Catalogue record for this book is available from the British Library.

ISBN 1 84538 497 0

Written by Honor Head
Consultant Chris Laurence, QVRM, TD, BCSc, MRCVS
Designed by Melissa Alaverdy
Editor Louisa Somerville
Pictures supplied by Warren Photographic

Publisher Steve Evans
Editorial Director Jean Coppendale
Art Director Zeta Davies

Printed and bound in China

Pedigree... or mongrel?

A Siamese cat has a sleek, long body and short fur. It has a long, pointed face.

Pedigree cats are specially bred for certain **characteristics**, such as length and colour of fur, face shape and eye colour. Siamese, Persians and Rex cats are all examples of pedigrees. Pedigree cats have parents that are the same breed. Mongrel cats are of mixed breed and the father is usually unknown. Their fur can be a variety of colours.

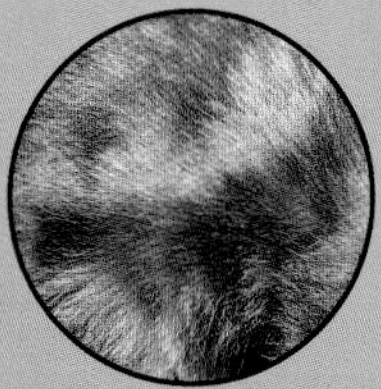

Tortoiseshell

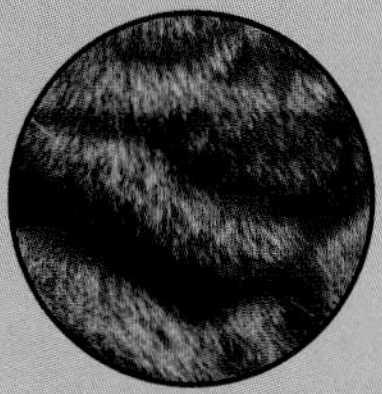

Tabby

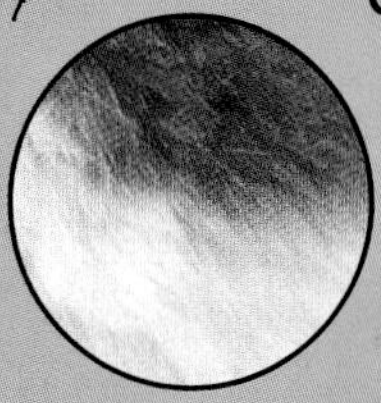

Ginger and white

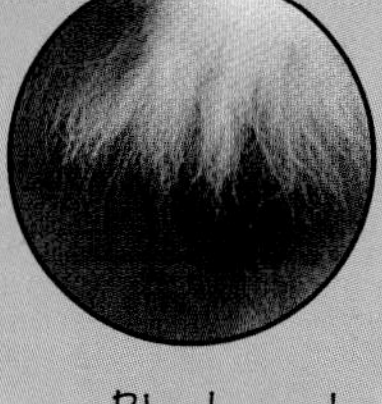

Black and white

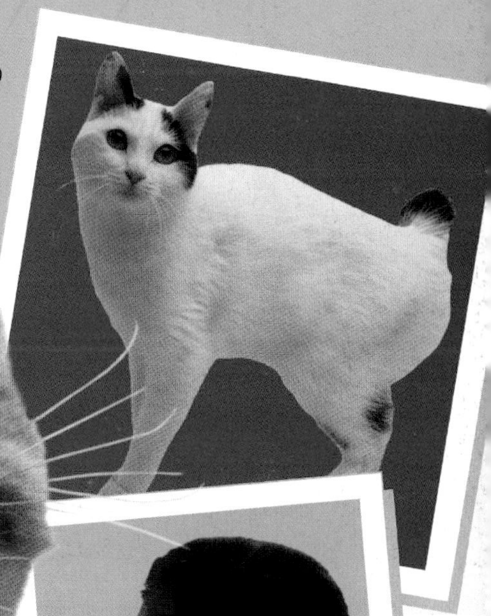

The Japanese Bobtail is a breed from Japan. It has a small round tail like a pom-pom.

Persian cats have long, silky fur. They also have a flat face with a short nose.

The Scottish Fold has small ears that fold forwards. The first ever Scottish Fold was born in a litter in Scotland, in 1961.

5

Pet cats are part of the same family as lions, tigers and other big cats. Thousands of years ago, before cats started living with people, they lived in the wild. They would hunt for food, defend their territory and fight off any competitors they met.

This is a statue of the Ancient Egyptian cat goddess Bast.

The first cats at home

The first known pictures of cats living with humans are from Ancient Egypt. They show cats with people either out hunting or at home. The Ancient Egyptians had a cat god called Bast and loved their pet cats so much that when one died, people would shave off their eyebrows as a mark of respect! They believed that cats were **reincarnations** of gods and often had their pets **mummified**.

A leopard is one of many big cats that live in the wild. It has excellent eyesight – just like your pet cat!

Wild streak

Even domestic (pet) cats are still hunters. Nearly all cats, wild or domestic, crouch down to stalk their **prey**. The cat keeps its body low to the ground to stay hidden in the bushes or grass. It moves quietly closer and closer to the prey until it's safe to pounce. Then it moves quickly and kills the prey. Excellent eyesight helps a cat to judge how far away the prey is and how big it is.

You might find that your pet crouches down like a wild cat when you play games with it!

Tooth and claw

Like its wild cousin, a domestic cat has long, dagger-like canine teeth which it uses to kill prey. Cats cannot chew their food so they use their back teeth, called molars, to cut it into chunks that they swallow whole. Both domestic and wild cats use their claws for grooming, climbing, protecting themselves and hunting. When a cat sharpens its claws on a scratching post (or on a tree), it is stretching and strengthening its muscles at the same time, helping to keep them supple.

Domestic and wild cats have similar long canine teeth.

Toilet secrets

When your cat goes to the toilet, it will usually bury whatever it has done. Wild cats do this to cover up any smells that might lead dangerous predators their way. Your pet isn't surrounded by hungry enemies at home, but it can't help behaving in the same way as its distant relatives.

Super senses

Your pet cat has incredible senses including night vision, excellent hearing and a great sense of smell. These skills were originally developed for hunting and surviving in the wild.

Bright eyes

One of the most amazing things about a cat's eyes is the way they glow in the dark, like car headlights. They shine because they reflect light, which helps the cat to see when it is semi-dark. In the wild, a cat would normally hunt at night or dusk and it needs to be able to see what it is chasing.

A cat on the prowl at night can see far more than a human can, but it cannot see in total darkness.

What's that noise?

Your cat has highly sensitive hearing, which is why it will hear a visitor at the front door long before you do. In the wild, your cat would notice the slightest sound, such as the rustle of a mouse or bird. A cat can swivel each ear separately to pick up where a sound is coming from and judge how far away it is. Cats are also good at remembering different sounds. This is why they come when you call them. They recognize the tone of your voice and the sound of their own name.

Cats can move each ear in a different direction. They can also pick up high-pitched sounds that humans cannot hear.

The cat's whiskers

A cat's whiskers are thick hairs that are super-sensitive to any small movement in the air. During the day, a cat uses its whiskers to judge whether gaps are wide enough for it to squeeze through. At night, a cat can use its whiskers to guide itself around objects in the dark by 'feeling' where things are.

Scent trails

Both wild and pet cats use scent to mark their territory. Their paws and heads have sweat glands that release scent. When a cat rubs its head against, or scratches, a tree or a piece of furniture it leaves its own unique smell behind. It might also spray urine. Scent trails pass information — such as how many other cats have been in the area and how long ago — from one cat to another.

When you feed your cat, stroke it and make it feel safe and comfortable. This is what a mother cat does for her kittens. After a while your pet will treat you as it would its own mother, or another friendly cat.

Saying 'hello'

When friendly cats meet, they rub up against each other to pick up each other's scent. When a cat rubs itself around your legs it is passing its scent onto you and making you one of its group. When you bend down and stroke your pet's head, it may rub the side of its face against your hand. It is passing on its scent from glands at the corner of its mouth. You may also notice that when you greet your cat, it stands on its hind legs. It's trying to get closer to your head to give you a friendly head rub, as mother cats do with their kittens.

Your cat will leave its scent on you as part of its way of saying 'hello'.

Getting comfy

Most cats knead with their paws before settling down onto a comfy lap or cushion. This is what kittens do to their mother's belly when they are first born, to encourage their mother to feed them milk. Some cats also dribble when they knead and may even start to suck your clothing. This is your pet returning to its kittenhood and thinking you're its mother!

When a cat kneads, it means it's feeling safe and secure.

A gift for you

Many pets will bring home a dead mouse or bird and leave it somewhere for you to find as a present. No matter how well fed your cat is, it will still hunt and want to share its catch with you. Kittens are taught how to kill prey by their mother. Your presents might be alive, rather than dead, if the kitten was taken away from its mother before she taught it the killing action. You could attach a bell to your cat's collar to avoid any unwanted gifts.

If your pet brings you a present, thank your cat and stroke it. Then ask an adult to pick up the dead animal and throw it away.

Will my cat get jealous?

Just like people, individual cats all react differently to new situations. Take care when you introduce your new cat to another pet that already lives with you. They may not like having a new animal in their territory and this could lead to fights. If a cat or dog that is used to attention is suddenly ignored because of the new arrival, it may also feel rejected.

11

Cat talk

As you get to know your pet you will notice that it has many different ways of expressing its feelings, especially through body language. Watch carefully and try to understand what your cat is telling you.

Tell tails

A cat mainly shows how it is feeling using its tail. When your pet walks towards you with its tail straight up in the air, it is saying 'hello'. It will walk around your legs and will like you to stroke its head and say its name. If a cat thrashes its tail from side to side, has its ears flat against its head or is hissing or spitting, it is angry or scared. Don't go near your cat when it's like this. Leave it alone until it has calmed down or call an adult to see what is wrong. If your cat moves its tail gently from side to side, it means it is relaxed and probably ready to sleep or play.

When cats fight they fluff up their fur and arch their backs to make themselves look bigger and taller.

Your cat will come to say a friendly 'hello' with its tail held high.

Ear signals

If your cat is sitting up and looking alert with it's ears upright, it is probably listening to a small noise that you can't hear. When your cat is playing with a toy, you will see it turn its ears towards the toy. It's listening for tiny noises or squeaks, just like it would if it was catching a mouse.

When you play with your pet, notice how it uses its ears and tail.

Meow!

Everyone knows that cats meow, but cats make a lot of other noises that you can learn to recognize. Your cat may chirrup when it is stroked, meow when it is hungry and growl or hiss if it is unhappy.

The mysterious purr

Purring is the noise kittens make when they are kneading their mother's belly and asking for milk. For both mother and kitten it is a comforting sound. Some cats purr for the rest of their lives, other cats don't purr at all but no one really knows why. Cats often purr when they are happy, but they also purr when they are in pain or distressed.

Listen to the sounds your cat makes and see how many different noises you can recognize.

13

Choosing a cat

Now that you know a bit more about cats, do you still think that a kitten is the right pet for you? Remember that a cat is a living creature with feelings and a personality. Kittens are small and fragile, they can be easily injured and frightened. Would you be a kind and gentle owner?

Where to look

The best place to go when choosing a pet cat is an animal rescue centre. They usually have lots of animals looking for good homes. The animals will have been well cared for and **neutered** and **vaccinated** by a vet.

Pedigree?

If you want to buy a pedigree cat then you should find a recommended **breeder**. Look in specialist cat magazines or on the internet, or ask your local vet. Avoid pet shops as there's no guarantee that the animals have been properly looked after and you can't be certain where they've come from. If you do go to a pet shop, ask your vet for advice first.

The people working at animal rescue centres will give you lots of advice on the best cat for you and how to look after it.

Which breed?

If you decide to buy a pedigree cat, ask your vet which sort would be best for you. Some breeds are better with children than others. Your vet will also tell you which breeds are easiest to look after. Whether you get a pedigree or a mongrel, think carefully before choosing a longhair. They need daily grooming. If you, or someone else in the family, can't keep up the grooming routine, their fur will quickly become matted. This could lead to distressing trips to the vet.

The best age for a kitten to leave its mother is between ten and twelve weeks old.

What to look for

When choosing your pet, look for a kitten or cat that has a shiny coat, clear eyes and a clean nose and bottom. Choose a kitten that seems friendly, bright and alert. Pick up the kitten or cat and see how it reacts to you. If it seems scared or timid and you have a noisy family, is it the right kitten for you? If the kitten is keen to play…and so are you… then maybe it's the one!

Should a stray stay?

What should you do if a strange cat turns up on your doorstep? It may have been reported lost, so ask your vet to check to see if it has a **microchip** (see page 26). Check trees, lampposts and newsagents' windows for 'lost' posters and put a notice in your local newspaper's 'found' column. If it is a lost cat and no one claims it, you can keep it as a pet, but if the owner turns up later to claim it, you must give it back. Take the cat to the vet to make sure that it has been neutered and is in good health. If it seems timid or scared, it is probably a **feral** cat. Give it food outside and ask your local cat rescue centre to come and take it. It is hard to live with a cat that is truly feral, and it may be ill or injured.

15

Getting ready

Part of the fun of having a new pet is preparing for its arrival. You need to make sure that the house is completely safe for your cat, decide on the best spot for feeding it and where it is going to sleep.

Making it safe

Cats, especially kittens, love to explore new surroundings. They get in and under everything. Make sure there are no poisonous plants in your home or garden that your pet can chew. Keep trailing plants and electrical wires out of reach of a playful kitten. Bottles of disinfectant and other chemicals should be put away in cupboards. If you are getting a kitten, cover any holes in floorboards that could lead to small spaces where your pet might get stuck. Fix gaps in the fence or front gate so your kitten cannot get lost or run into the street. If you have an open fire, put up a fireguard so your kitten doesn't race up the chimney. Outside, make sure the shed or garage door is firmly shut.

elephant's ears

sweet pea

poinsettias

oleander

Some cats will chew plants, so make sure that you do not have any poisonous plants in your house or garden.

Space to sleep and eat

Decide where your pet will eat, sleep and have its litter tray. Put its bed somewhere private, away from draughts. Buy a proper bed or put a blanket or cushion in a shallow cardboard box. Your pet should have a food bowl and a water bowl. Put them somewhere quiet so your cat can eat in peace. It's a good idea to put a special plastic mat under the bowls as many cats pull their food out of the bowl before eating it!

Always give your pet somewhere to sleep... but it will probably find its own favourite place to nap as well.

Litter tray

The litter tray should be in the same room as the food bowls and sleeping basket – but not too close. Put the litter tray somewhere quiet. Spread out newspaper underneath, too, as **cat litter** always ends up outside the tray.

Checklist

Here is a checklist of things you might want to buy for your new pet:

🐾 A cat flap

🐾 Travel basket

🐾 Two bowls: one for water, one for food

🐾 Food

🐾 Plastic food mat

🐾 Litter tray

🐾 Bag of cat litter

🐾 Litter scoop

🐾 Basket or box for a bed

🐾 Veterinary fleece for bed

🐾 A scratching post

🐾 If it is a longhaired cat, you will need the right sort of combs and brushes

🐾 Toys – if you're getting a kitten, toys must not have small parts that could come off and be swallowed

🐾 Collar – cats really don't need collars but if you do buy one, choose a snap–apart collar

Welcome to your new home

Your new pet will feel nervous about moving into its new surroundings. Spend plenty of time with your cat during the first few days to help it feel safe. You can even buy a special product from your vet that releases a scent into the air which will help your new cat to settle in.

The first few days

Your pet will start to get used to all the new smells by sniffing at the furniture – and the family. Shut all windows and doors to unsafe rooms, such as garages. Show your pet its food bowls, litter tray and sleeping basket. Make sure there is water in its bowl. Don't give your pet milk, as this can make some cats very ill. Talk quietly to your pet and say its name, so that it gets to know the sound of your voice. Give it some toys to play with. Don't let your cat out of doors until it has been vaccinated and microchipped (see page 26). Don't let it out in very cold weather, either. Restrict your pet to one or two rooms, until it is used to you and your home's new smells.

Stay with your pet for the first couple of hours to make sure it doesn't get into trouble or feel lonely. Stroke and play with it, but be gentle.

Food and sleep

Gently place your cat next to its food bowls and give it some solid food. Kittens should have small meals of kitten food about four to six times a day. Adult cats need two meals a day and pedigree cats may have special feeding needs. Cats can become ill if they eat only vegetarian food, so they should be given meat every day. Once your pet has eaten, show it the litter tray. When your cat has finished, praise it and put it in its bed.

Tasty treats

It's all right to give your pet a treat every now and again, but never let it get too fat. Some cats like cheese, cake or prawns – you'll soon get to know your pet's favourites. Don't give your cat chicken or pork bones, or fish with bones, as they could choke it. If you have more than one pet, each animal should have its own food bowl. Don't feed your pet cold food straight from the fridge. Wild cats eat food freshly killed and still warm, so your pet cat will like its food at body temperature.

Other pets

If you have any caged pets such as rabbits, gerbils or guinea pigs, make sure the cat can't reach the cage. Only introduce your new pet to other cats or dogs in the house after the first day or so. Don't leave them alone together until you're sure they won't fight. If they do fight a lot, or one of them stops eating or starts to behave in a strange way – such as messing in the house – talk to your vet about it.

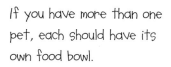

If you have more than one pet, each should have its own food bowl.

You must treat your pet kindly and with respect. If you handle your pet properly from the start, it will learn to trust you and you'll have a friend for life.

Handle with care

Never hit your cat, throw things at it or shout at it. Stroke it gently from its head to its tail, never in the other direction. Don't pull its tail or whiskers and avoid making sudden movements near your pet, especially when it is young, as you may scare it. A cat has very sharp claws and will lash out if it's frightened or thinks it's being attacked. Your pet also has sharp teeth and will bite if it thinks you're going to harm it.

Talk quietly to your pet when you stroke it, and say its name.

Most cats enjoy being scratched behind the ears and on the top of the head but they don't like their back legs or paws to be touched. Be very gentle if you stroke its tummy and only do this when you have got to know your pet. If it doesn't like it, stop.

Picking up

To pick your cat up, put one arm around its chest and under its front legs. Use the other hand to scoop up and support its back legs. Hold it against your body but don't squeeze it tightly. Always turn your face away in case it lashes out with its paw. If your pet starts to struggle, don't force it to stay in your arms. Put it down immediately. Don't drop it, place it on the floor carefully.

When you hold your cat, never squeeze it.

It's not a toy!

Never let your cat's legs hang down when you carry it and don't pick it up by the **scruff** of its neck. Mother cats do this when their kittens are tiny and light. Older, heavier cats will get hurt. Don't try to dress up your cat and don't chase it, which is dangerous for both of you! Never lock it in a box or cupboard.

Brush and comb

Buy proper cat brushes and combs and brush from the head towards the tail, and from the base of the tail to the tip. Some cats love having their tummy brushed too, but take care as yours may not. Most cats like being groomed but if your cat doesn't, don't force it unless you have a longhair. It's vital that longhaired cats are groomed regularly so talk to your vet if there's a problem.

Talk to your cat as you groom it and when it has had enough, let it go.

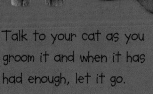

21

House rules

Before you get your new pet, you should decide what it will and won't be allowed to do. The naughty antics of a kitten may seem cute but will soon become annoying once the kitten is a full-grown cat.

It is very difficult to break bad habits once they have been allowed to develop.

Bad habits

Cats love scratching furniture, jumping up on tables and high places, begging at the table, demanding to be fed and sleeping in comfy spots such as your bed! But you can train your pet into good habits by giving it rewards. For example, to get your cat to come when you call, give it a treat, such as food or lots of fuss, each time it responds. If your pet does something good, always stroke and praise it.

Training tips

To stop your cat getting into bad habits, start its training early on. If it jumps on the table or chairs, gently lift it down and say "No" in a firm voice. If there is a chair that you don't mind it sleeping on, move it there. If it scratches, say "No". Pick it up and put it beside its scratching post. You can clap your hands, too, or bang a rolled-up newspaper on the floor next to it. Cats hate sudden noises and this should be enough to stop the naughty behaviour. If you really can't break your cat's bad habits, speak to your vet. Never hit your pet.

When your cat uses its scratching post, praise your pet and stroke it.

Toilet training

Your cat should go to the toilet out of doors or use a litter tray. If your cat messes outside its tray, check the cat litter is clean, or try a different brand. Some cats may mess if they have been upset or have an infection, in which case take your pet to the vet. If your pet usually uses the garden but starts to mess in the house, another cat may be bullying it, so give your pet a litter tray. If your pet messes in the house but you don't find the mess until later, don't tell it off because it won't understand why.

Regular feeding

Feed your pet at the same time each day and don't give it food at other times. If it comes into the kitchen meowing for food, ignore it and it will soon find somewhere to curl up for a snooze until its proper meal time. If you want give your pet a treat, put it inside or next to your cat's bowl at a meal time.

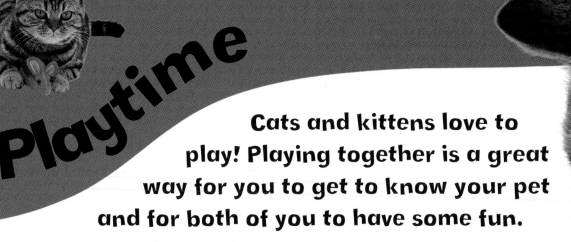

Playtime

Cats and kittens love to play! Playing together is a great way for you to get to know your pet and for both of you to have some fun.

Make a playground

Kittens and young cats are bursting with curiosity, so make interesting places for your pet to explore. Cut holes of different shapes in cardboard boxes or leave the lids open, but make sure that there are no sharp edges. Find small soft balls to play with. Roll them into or around a box and watch your pet go in search of them. When playing with a kitten, make sure the ball is not so small that your pet could swallow it. It's best to buy special pet toys that have been safety tested.

Cats use their hunting instincts when they play with toys.

Kittens love exploring old boxes.

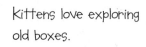

Safe toys

You can easily make some safe toys for your pet. Tie a feather or a safety-tested toy mouse to a piece of string. Dangle it in front of your pet, or pull it along the floor. See how your pet uses its hunting instincts to play with the pretend prey. Scrunch up some newspaper and roll the paper ball along the floor. Make sure that where you are playing is safe, check that there are no sharp corners and nothing to knock over. Always play with your kitten on the floor so it doesn't fall off anything and hurt itself.

Catnip crazy

Catnip is a herb with a scent that cats adore! You can grow it in the garden or in a pot. Some cats will roll around, make noises and act quite strangely when they come across it. Most cats will at least go up and have a good sniff at it. Many cat toys are filled with catnip to encourage the cat to play with them. Try hiding a few catnip toys around your house to see if your cat can track them down. Catnip won't harm your pet.

Food hunt

If your cat stays in most of the time, it will especially enjoy a food hunt. Hide small amounts of dried food in some of the cat's play boxes or on top of its scratching post and watch it sniff out the food.

Going to the vet

When you first get your kitten you should take it to the vet for a check-up. It should have vaccinations against illnesses, such as cat flu and feline enteritis. You should also ask the vet if your pet needs to be wormed. This means giving it some special tablets to kill any worms it may have.

Microchipping

Ask the vet about microchipping. A microchip is smaller than a grain of rice and can be painlessly inserted under your pet's skin. Every microchip has its own unique number. When a lost cat is found, the vet can use a scanner to 'read' the number and then look up the owner's name, address and telephone number on a computer database.

If your cat has a microchip you have a better chance of finding your pet if it gets lost.

Spaying and neutering

Male cats should be neutered, and females should be spayed, so that they can't have kittens. Male cats looking for females often wander off and risk getting lost or having an accident. They might also get injured fighting other male cats. Unless you and your family are prepared to look after kittens, it is unfair to let your female pet cat have a litter.

Furballs and fleas

Cats that have long or semi-long fur may get furballs. When a cat licks itself, it swallows a lot of fur, which creates a ball in its stomach. Usually the fur ball passes through the cat when it goes to the toilet, or it vomits it up. If you groom your cat daily, it will help to stop it swallowing too much fur. While you are grooming your pet you might notice small black flea droppings, or even see a flea running through its fur. Ask the vet for some flea treatment. Never leave fleas untreated or they will get worse and make your pet unhappy.

Cats are very clean animals that groom themselves a lot.

Cat manicure

As well as licking its fur, you may see your cat pulling at its back claws. Cats do this when the claw sheath (covering) has grown too long. They pull off the old sheath, just as we cut our nails when they get too long.

Cats keep their front claws short by scratching, but their back claws don't get worn down so they have to bite the sheath off.

Odd behaviour

If something upsets your pet, such as being bullied by another cat or a change in its routine, it might behave in a strange way. For example, it may mess in the house, make howling noises at night or hide when it sees you coming. Keep a note of all the unusual behaviour and when it started to happen, so that you can tell your vet. It could be a sign of illness, so it's always worth checking.

Your elderly cat

As your pet gets older you will see signs of ageing. Older cats become thinner, their fur starts to go grey and they may slow down and go out less. However, many cats stay bright and alert and enjoy playing well into old age.

Health problems

Older cats hear and see less and sleep more. They can get arthritis, which makes their joints stiff and painful, so an older pet will need a soft bed on the ground, away from draughts. Older cats' teeth can also become weak and loose, making it hard for them to eat. If your pet suddenly starts to drink more water than usual, this could be a sign that it has kidney problems or diabetes. If you think there is anything wrong with your pet, take it to the vet for a check-up immediately.

Like humans, cats look different as they get older. These two pictures are of the same cat, young and old.

28

Keep talking

An elderly cat will still like to be stroked but may not want to be picked up if its joints are stiff. Instead, kneel down beside your pet. It will probably still enjoy playing with a piece of string or rolled-up paper. If your pet becomes ill, make a bed for it somewhere warm and safe. If it is unable to go out, it will need a litter tray nearby.

Saying goodbye

If your pet is very ill or in pain it may have to be put down. The vet will give it an injection so that it dies painlessly. You can talk to your pet while the vet gives it the injection. After your cat has died you could bring it home and bury it in a special place in the garden. Or your vet may cremate your pet and then you can scatter the ashes in your garden or the park. You could have a ceremony to say goodbye.

How old is your cat?

A cat ages faster than a human. A two-year-old cat is as old as a person of 25 years! Here is a rough chart of cat years compared with human years.

Cat	1	2	6	10	14	20
Human	15	25	45	60	72	95

Older cats enjoy company just as much as kittens and should not be ignored or neglected.

Remembering your pet

Everyone understands how sad it is when a pet dies, so talk to your friends and family about your cat. If you feel like crying, don't be embarrassed. You could write a story, look at some old photographs or make a scrapbook about your pet's life.

Make a collage using your favourite picture of your cat.

29

Glossary

breed	A type of pedigree cat, such as a Siamese or Persian
breeder	Someone who makes a living from breeding certain types of pedigree cats
cat litter	Granules, or bits, that go in a litter tray (a cat's indoor toilet)
characteristic	A physical feature such as long or short fur or eye colour
feral	A wild animal that is not tamed or trained
groom	To keep fur clean and tangle free
litter	A group of kittens born at the same time
microchip	An electronic chip inserted under a pet's skin
mongrel	A mixed breed cat
mummify	To embalm a dead body and turn it into a mummy
neuter	An operation to stop male animals breeding
pedigree	A cat bred from two cats that share the same features, such as face shape and hair length
reincarnation	The belief that when you die, you are reborn as another person or animal
scruff	Loose skin around an animal's neck
spay	An operation to stop female animals breeding
vaccination	An injection that can prevent an animal catching a disease

Index

Notes for parents

- The adults in the family are legally responsible for the safety, care and well-being of any pets.

- All pets are expensive and time consuming. Be sure you have the money and time to look after a pet. Vets' bills are expensive, so it may be worthwhile investigating pet insurance.

- Never leave young children and pets alone together. A cat may not be a suitable pet for a very young child or a noisy or boisterous child.

- Both male and female cats should be neutered at the age of about four to five months.

- Always make sure your children wash their hands after grooming a cat or cleaning its litter tray or food bowls.

- If a child is scratched, clean the wound with disinfectant. If a child is bitten, contact your doctor for advice as cat bites can cause nasty infections.